MIGHTY MACHINES

Backhoes

by Ray McClellan

BELLWETHER MEDIA • MINNEAPOLIS, MN

Note to Librarians, Teachers, and Parents:

Blastoff! Readers are carefully developed by literacy experts and combine standards-based content with developmentally appropriate text.

Level 1 provides the most support through repetition of high-frequency words, light text, predictable sentence patterns, and strong visual support.

Level 2 offers early readers a bit more challenge through varied simple sentences, increased text load, and less repetition of high-frequency words.

Level 3 advances early-fluent readers toward fluency through increased text and concept load, less reliance on visuals, longer sentences, and more literary language.

Whichever book is right for your reader, Blastoff! Readers are the perfect books to build confidence and encourage a love of reading that will last a lifetime!

This edition first published in 2007 by Bellwether Media.

No part of this publication may be reproduced in whole or in part without written permission of the publisher. For information regarding permission, write to Bellwether Media Inc., Attention: Permissions Department, Post Office Box 1C, Minnetonka, MN 55345-9998.

Library of Congress Cataloging-in-Publication Data
McClellan, Ray.
  Backhoes / by Ray McClellan.
    p. cm. — (Blastoff! readers) (Mighty machines)
Summary: "Simple text and supportive images introduce young readers to backhoes. Intended for students in kindergarten through third grade."
  Includes bibliographical references and index.
  ISBN-10: 1-60014-042-4 (hardcover : alk. paper)
  ISBN-13: 978-1-60014-042-6 (hardcover : alk. paper)
  1. Backhoes—Juvenile literature. I. Title. II. Series. III. Series: Mighty machines (Bellwether Media)

TA735.M452 2006
629.225—dc22   2006007216

Text copyright © 2007 by Bellwether Media.
Printed in the United States of America.

Table of Contents

The backhoe is
a big machine.
It digs and moves
heavy **loads**.

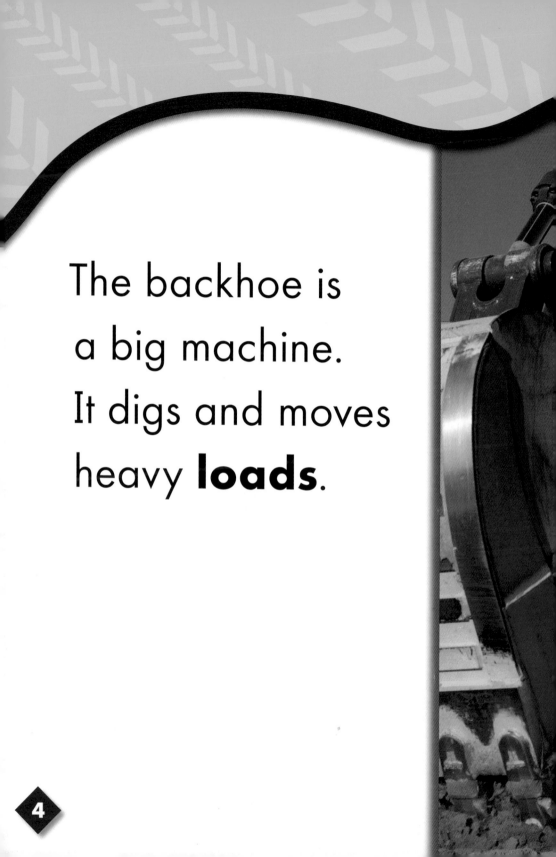

The backhoe has a **cab**. A worker sits in the cab.

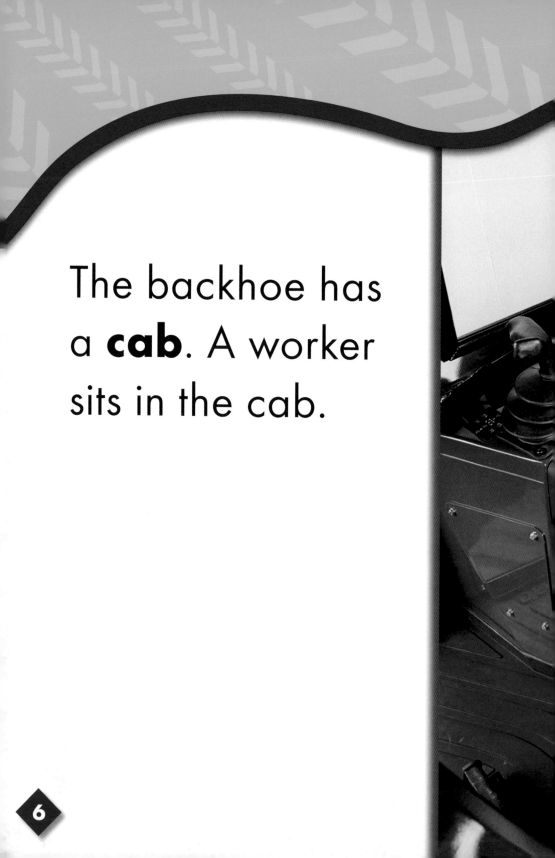

The backhoe has a long **boom**. The boom has a **digging bucket**.

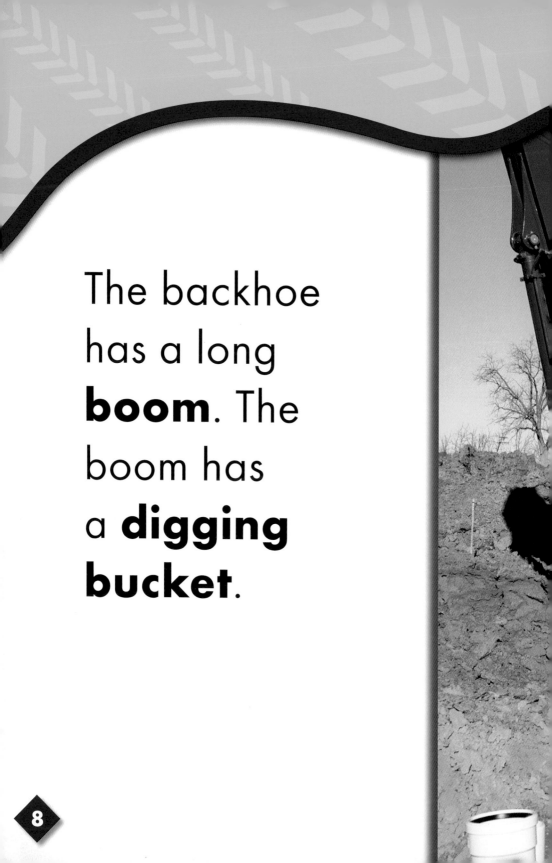

boom

digging bucket

The bucket
digs up dirt
and rocks.

This backhoe drops the dirt and rocks into a dump truck.

DEERE

400

Some backhoes have two buckets. The smaller bucket digs up dirt.

The bigger bucket carries and dumps the dirt.

Some backhoes have **tracks**. Tracks work well on sand and mud.

tracks →

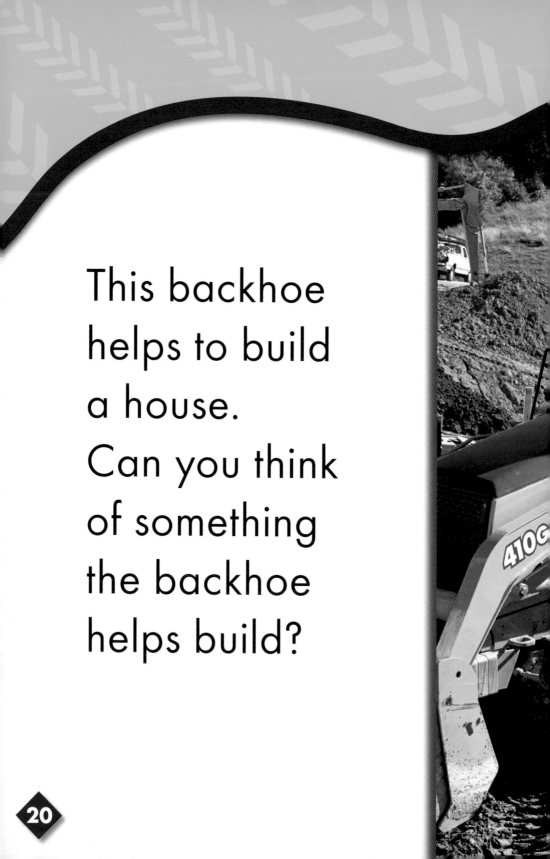

This backhoe helps to build a house. Can you think of something the backhoe helps build?

Glossary

boom—a metal arm that connects to the backhoe bucket

cab—the place where a worker sits

digging bucket—a large scoop at the end of the boom

load—anything that is carried or lifted by a machine or a person

tracks—a wide belt made of metal or rubber that helps the backhoe to move

To Learn More

AT THE LIBRARY

Deschamps, Nicola. *Digger*. New York: DK Publishing, 2004.

Jones, Melanie Davis. *Big Machines*. New York: Children's Press, 2003.

Randolph, Joanne. *Backhoes*. New York: Powerkids Press, 2002.

ON THE WEB

Learning more about mighty machines is as easy as 1, 2, 3.

1. Go to www.factsurfer.com

2. Enter "mighty machines" into search box.

3. Click the "Surf" button and you will see a list of related web sites.

With factsurfer.com, finding more information is just a click away.

Index